D1123862

T2-BVG-267

# CATS

BY M. C. SWENSEN

PUBLISHED BY THE CHILD'S WORLD®

**The Child's World®**
childsworld.com

Published by The Child's World®
1980 Lookout Drive • Mankato, MN 56003-1705
800-599-READ • www.childsworld.com

*For Gracie and Willy.*

ACKNOWLEDGMENTS
The Child's World®: Mary Swensen, Publishing Director
The Design Lab: Design
Michael Miller: Editing
Sarah M. Miller: Editing

DESIGN ELEMENTS
© Doremi/Shutterstock.com

PHOTO CREDITS
© ANCH/Shutterstock.com: 6-7; Anna Ri/Shutterstock.com:
cover; FXQuadro/Shutterstock.com: 5; hannadarzy/Shutterstock.
com: 12; Irina Kozorog/Shutterstock.com: 16-17; Maly Designer/
Shutterstock.com: 10; Misollia/Dreamstime.com: 9; Orhan Cam/
Shutterstock.com: 15; Robynrg/Shutterstock.com: 19; Scharfsinn/
Shutterstock.com: 20-21

ISBN: 9781503808232
LCCN: 2015958483

Printed in the United States of America
Mankato, MN
June, 2016
PA02308

# Table of Contents

## Cute Cats

"Meow!" What is that cat saying? Cats can be big or small. They have four legs and two ears. They have a long tail. Cats have a little nose and long **whiskers**.

**DID YOU KNOW?**

MOST PET CATS WEIGH BETWEEN 5 AND 20 POUNDS (2 AND 9 KILOGRAMS).

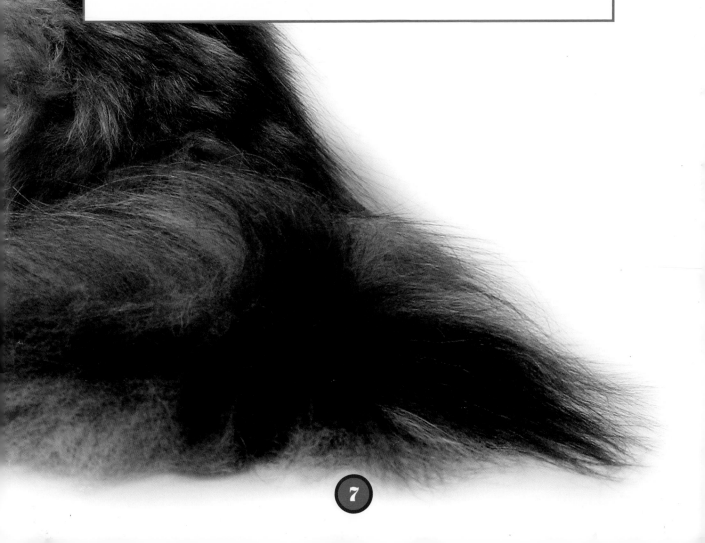

Most cats are covered in soft hair. Some cats have long hair. Others do not have any hair at all!

# Many Colors

Cats can be many colors. Most cats are white, black, gray, or brown. Some cats are just one color. Other cats have stripes or spots.

**DID YOU KNOW?**

CATS HAVE ABOUT 24 WHISKERS ON THEIR FACE.

SOME CATS HAVE MORE. SOME HAVE LESS.

## Keeping Clean

Cats lick their body to keep clean. Their tongue is rough and bumpy. The bumps act like a brush. They remove dirt and old hair.

**DID YOU KNOW?**

SOME CATS CAN JUMP FIVE TIMES THEIR OWN HEIGHT.

# Claws

Cats have sharp claws. They have five claws on each of their front feet. There are four claws on each of their back feet. Cats use their claws to climb and scratch.

# Baby Cats

Baby cats are called **kittens**. They cannot see when they are born. They do not open their eyes until they are nine days old. Kittens drink milk from their mother.

**DID YOU KNOW?**

CATS CAN MAKE MORE THAN 100 SOUNDS.

15

# Eating

Adult cats eat meat foods. Pet cats eat cat food from a store. It has meat flavors. The food can be wet or dry. Cats also like fresh water to drink.

# Hunting

Some cats hunt for mice or birds. They stay low and **crouch**. They sneak quietly. Then they pounce!

**DID YOU KNOW?**

CATS ARE ABLE TO SEE VERY WELL IN THE DARK.

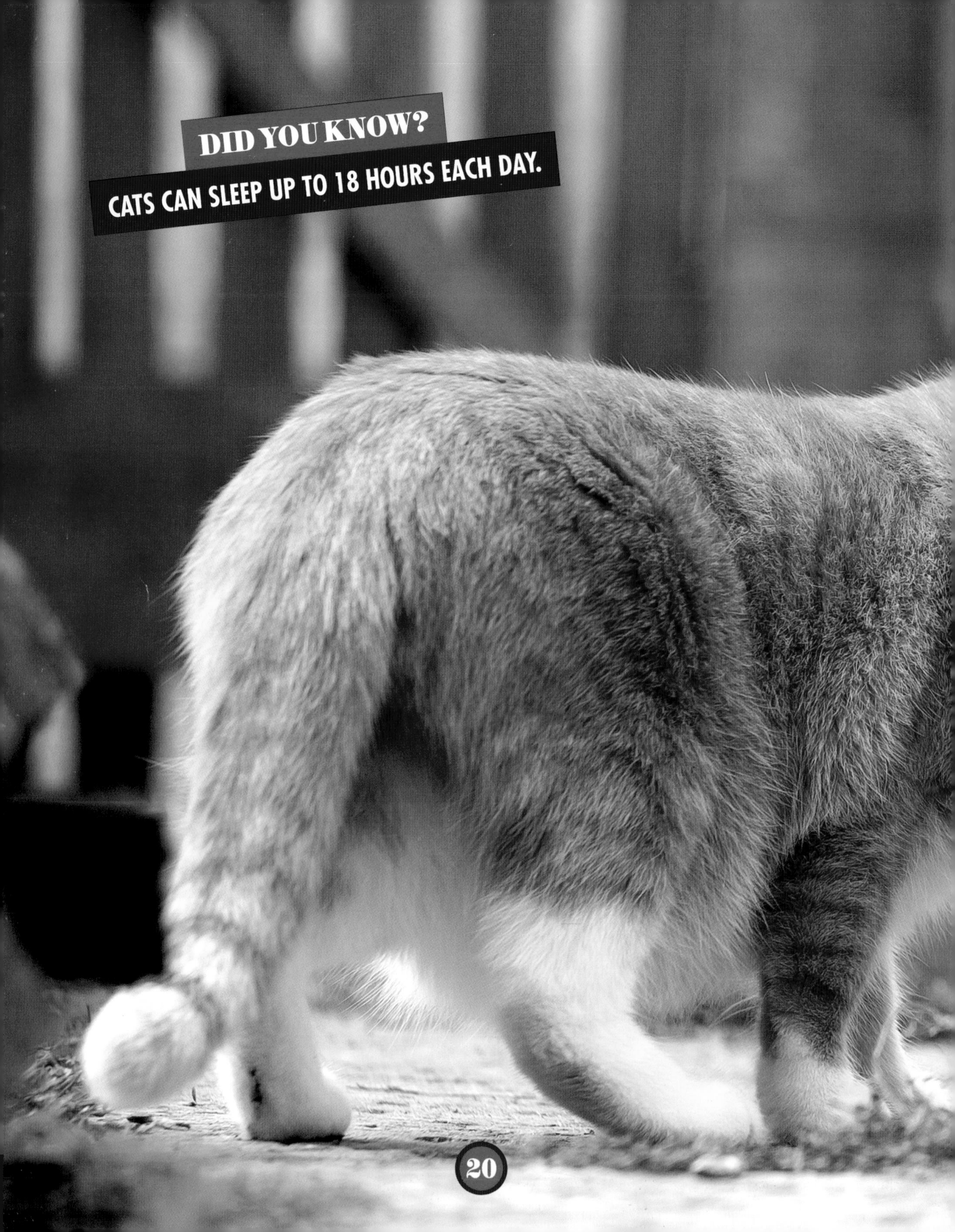

## DID YOU KNOW?

CATS CAN SLEEP UP TO 18 HOURS EACH DAY.

Cats are smart and gentle. They like to play and hunt. Would you like a pet cat?

# Glossary

**CLOWDER** (KLOW-dur) A clowder is a group of cats.

**CROUCH** (KROWCH) To crouch is to lower your body and bend your legs.

**KITTENS** (KIT-tenz) Kittens are baby cats.

**WHISKERS** (WHIS-kerz) Whiskers are long, stiff hairs that some animals have on their face.

# To Learn More

### IN THE LIBRARY

Crisp, Marty. *Everything Cat: What Kids Really Want to Know about Cats*. Chanhassen, MN: NorthWord Press, 2003.

Holub, Joan. *Why Do Cats Meow?* Mineola, NY: Dover Publications, 2011.

Stevens, Kathryn. *Cats*. Mankato, MN: The Child's World, 2016.

### ON THE WEB

Visit our Web site for links about cats:
**childsworld.com/links**

Note to Parents, Teachers, and Librarians: We routinely verify our Web links to make sure they are safe and active sites. So encourage your readers to check them out!

# Index

## ABOUT THE AUTHOR

M. C. Swensen has lived in Minnesota all her life. When she's not reading or writing, M. C. enjoys spending time with her husband and dogs and traveling to interesting places.